General editor: Graham Han

Brodie's Notes on Jo

Paradise Lost
Books I and II

Ray Wilkinson

150th YEAR
M
MACMILLAN

First published 1978 by Pan Books Ltd

This revised edition published 1993 by
THE MACMILLAN PRESS LTD
Houndmills, Basingstoke, Hampshire RG21 2XS
and London
Companies and representatives
throughout the world

ISBN 0-333-58156-3

Typeset by Footnote Graphics, Warminster, Wiltshire
Printed in Great Britain by
Cox & Wyman Ltd, Reading

Contents

Preface

The intention throughout this study aid is to stimulate and guide, to encourage your involvement in the book, and to develop informed responses and a sure understanding of the main details.

Brodie's Notes provide a clear outline of the play or novel's plot, followed by act, scene, or chapter summaries and/or commentaries. These are designed to emphasize the most important literary and factual details. Poems, stories or non-fiction texts combine brief summary with critical commentary on individual aspects or common features of the genre being examined. Textual notes define what is difficult or obscure and emphasize literary qualities. Revision questions are set at appropriate points to test your ability to appreciate the prescribed book and to write accurately and relevantly about it.

In addition, each of these Notes includes a critical appreciation of the author's art. This covers such major elements as characterization, style, structure, setting and themes. Poems are examined technically – rhyme, rhythm, for instance. In fact, any important aspect of the prescribed work will be evaluated. The aim is to send you back to the text you are studying.

Each study aid concludes with a series of general questions which require a detailed knowledge of the book: some of these questions may invite comparison with other books, some will be suitable for coursework exercises, and some could be adapted to work you are doing on another book or books. Each study aid has been adapted to meet the needs of the current examination requirements. They provide a basic, individual and imaginative response to the work being studied, and it is hoped that they will stimulate you to acquire disciplined reading habits and critical fluency.

Graham Handley 1990

The author and his work

Milton was born in 1608, in London. His father, who had been disinherited for deserting the family's Catholic religion, was a scrivener – a scribe or copyist – whose hobby and dominating interest was music. From his earliest years Milton was an omnivorous reader. He attended St Paul's School and his studies were supplemented by a private tutor who taught him Hebrew, French and Italian, to add to the Greek and Latin which were, of course, the staple of Renaissance education. He learned to compose Latin verse, to think in Latin. He wrote Latin verse for much of his life and often reserved his most personal thoughts and emotions for that language. There was still a European audience for Latin poems, and if a poet was looking for world-wide fame he might be ill-advised to write in English. Even while Milton was still a child he and his father seem to have believed that he was chosen for some great work in learning and literature.

In 1625, shortly before the accession of Charles I, Milton went up to Christ's College, Cambridge. He seems to have been at odds with the authorities – a characteristic that remained with him for much of his life. He objected to the still-practised medieval system of education, based on disputation and scholastic logic, which Milton thought of as quibbling. But his work shows his own outstanding ability to argue a case, even a case in which he did not believe – for instance in his portrayal of Satan and Comus. He came to mistrust the art of rhetoric, which could easily degenerate into the art of convincing lying. Possibly because of his youthful appearance and personal fastidiousness, he was known as 'the lady of Christ's'. He wrote copiously at this time, in both Latin and English, the English poems including some assured elegies written before he was eighteen.

The 'Nativity Ode' ('On the Morning of Christ's Nativity' with 'The Hymn') was written in 1629; it is probably the best poem written in English by a young man of twenty-one. He experimented with different forms and languages, writing some poems in Italian. He took his MA degree in 1632 and then went to his father's estate at Horton in Buckinghamshire where he stayed for six years, studying and continuing to prepare himself for his vocation as a poet. Here he wrote 'At A Solemn Music', 'L'Allegro', 'Il Penseroso', 'A Mask' (Comus) and 'Lycidas', but even by the time he wrote 'Lycidas' (when he was nearly thirty), Milton still felt unready for his great work, whatever it was to be.

In 1638 he visited Italy, the centre of European civilization, and spent about sixteen months there. He later wrote that Italy was 'the lodging place of *humanitas* and all the arts of civilization'. He read his Latin and Italian poems at literary societies, where they were much admired.

He returned to England in the summer of 1639. The country was riven by related political and religious controversies. Milton became involved in writing pamphlets against the episcopacy, urging that the work of the Reformation should be finished, and in defence of liberty, 'religious, domestic and civil'. It seemed to be the dawning of a new glorious age, of which he hoped to be the poet, though – apart from a few sonnets – he was to write no poetry for nearly twenty years.

In 1643 he married Mary Powell, who was only sixteen. She left him about a month after their marriage, though she returned to him in 1645. He had obviously married totally unsuitably, and even before his wife left him he had begun to write *The Doctrine and Discipline of Divorce*, urging that incompatible partners should be allowed to divorce. In 1644 he wrote *Areopagitica*, in which he argued the value of the free publication of books, and that truth would eventually triumph over error.

Charles I was executed in 1649 and shortly afterwards Milton wrote *The Tenure of Kings and Magistrates*, justifying regicide. He was employed by Cromwell to justify the execution of the King – in Latin, to a European audience. At this time his eyesight began seriously to fail and by 1652 he was totally blind. Mary Powell died in 1655. He married Katherine Woodcock in 1656, but after a brief, happy marriage (see the Sonnet 'Methought I saw my late espoused saint') she died in childbirth in 1658.

Cromwell, whom Milton greatly admired, died in 1658 and the country fell under military rule. At the time of the Restoration in 1660 Milton was fifty-one years old, a blind and disappointed man. He was imprisoned for a short time and must have considered himself lucky when he was set free. He had begun to write *Paradise Lost* in 1655 and finished it, in retirement in the country, in 1663. The poem was published in 1667, and he was given an immediate payment of five pounds. The poem brought him a large measure of recognition, both from the more discerning of his countrymen and from foreigners who came to visit him. He also wrote a tragedy after the Greek model, *Samson Agonistes*; and *Paradise Regained*, a brief epic in four books, describing Christ's temptation in the wilderness in which Satan is overcome. He married again in 1663, and died eleven years later, in 1674.

Milton's verse

Milton's verse has a range of reference which is outside the scope of most modern readers – just as modern verse has a range of reference which would have completely baffled Milton. He was a learned man, and he used his learning. Few of us can understand his verse without frequent use of notes, and even these fail to convey the entire, spontaneously apprehended overtones which the poet intended. Short of becoming as learned as Milton there is no way round this, but there is no need to be discouraged; particularly when he is well read aloud, he still has a great deal to offer. In any case it is doubtful whether he is as difficult to understand as, say, Donne, or, because of his metaphorical complexity, Shakespeare.

In the last fifty years Milton's style has come under severe attack. Dr Johnson stated the matter succinctly in his *Life of Milton* when he said that Milton 'formed his style on a perverse and pedantic principle. He was desirous to use English words with a foreign idiom'. Dr F. R. Leavis, in a famous essay in *Revaluation* writes of what he calls 'the monotony of the ritual' in *Paradise Lost*, and, initially, he had support from T. S. Eliot. Dr Leavis said that 'mere orotundity is a disproportionate part of the effect', and T. S. Eliot argued that the words were arranged 'for the sake of musical value, not for significance'.

The defence of Milton against these charges has been roughly of two kinds: there have been those, like C. S. Lewis in *A Preface to Paradise Lost*, who have broadly accepted Dr Leavis's description of Milton's style, but have said that they liked it and found it appropriate to the epic; and there have been those, like Christopher Ricks in *Milton's Grand Style* who have attempted to show in detail the richness, variety and force of Milton's particular effects.

Milton does, undoubtedly, frequently twist the natural order of English words. Many of his sentences are long, and their grammar can be extraordinarily complex. The very first sentence of the poem is 120-odd words long, a giant leap into a giant subject. The actual words, however, are simple and strong, and the sentence is so constructed as to bring the emphasis down where he wants it and to drop the ideas into the reader's mind with just the weight or contrast which he intends; first the statement of the whole breadth of his theme; then the great emphasis on 'Sing' and the mimetic 'heavens and earth/Rose out of chaos'; last the unbroken, surging, confident rhythm of 'I thence ...' to 'Things unattempted yet in prose or rhyme'. The 'no middle flight' expresses and *enacts* the size and grandeur of his venture.

It ought to be added, however – obvious though it is – that Milton had no one single style; he believed that there was a style that was appropriate, 'answerable', for the subject of a particular poem, and in *Paradise Lost* it was natural that the style should be magniloquent. Moreover, even in *Paradise Lost*, Milton was also master of great simplicities, both of situation and of style, to which he repeatedly comes home. Here are just a few, chosen from Books I and II:

> I may assert eternal providence,
> And justify the ways of God to men ...
> Who durst defy the Omnipotent to arms ...
> ... What though the field be lost?
> Better to reign in Hell than serve in Heaven ...
> My sentence is for open war ...
> Which if not victory is yet revenge ...
>   ... What if we find
> Some easier enterprise?
> The dark unbottomed infinite abyss ...
> Where all life dies, death lives ...
> Accursed, and in a cursed hour he hies.

Many, many examples of such command of direct, pithy English can be found through the poem.

Perhaps the biggest difficulties in reading Milton are not the obvious ones, where we are plainly ignorant, but the subtler ones where we may think that we know what Milton means but are mistaken. Many words have changed their meanings over the centuries. For instance, 'buxom' used to mean 'pliant' or 'obedient'; today it means something more like 'pleasantly plump' and is generally used of girls. Perhaps it was thought that plump women were more likely to be obedient than thin ones. Milton lived much closer to the origin of words, particularly the *Latin* origin, than we do; and it is the usual habit of words to become weaker in meaning with the passage of time, either through overwork or misuse. For instance, Milton makes a good deal of use of 'horror' and 'horrid', and it is hard now to recapture the full sense of bristling hair standing on end. Similarly, 'abject' meant literally 'thrown down', 'admire' meant 'wonder', 'awful' meant 'inspiring awe and wonder', 'frequent' meant 'crowded', 'success' meant 'results', not necessarily 'good results', 'sentence' meant 'opinion', 'reluctance' meant 'forcible struggling against', and so on.

Finally, the difficulty of Milton is not that he is long-winded but that he is tight-packed. The best comment on this was perhaps made by Jonathan Richardson in his *Explanatory Notes on Paradise Lost*, written in 1734: 'The reader of Milton must be always up on duty; he is surrounded with sense, it rises in every line, every word is to the purpose; it has all been considered, and demands, and merits, observation ... Milton's (sentences) are all substance and weight. If this be called obscurity, let it be remembered that it is such an obscurity as is a compliment to the reader; not that vicious obscurity which proceeds from a muddled head'.

Milton's puritanism

This is a large subject, and only a few observations can be made here.

Puritanism is sometimes associated with a fierce distrust of pleasure of all kinds and Milton can sometimes appear – and be – austere and intolerant. What emerges from *Paradise Lost* is his distrust of pleasure and even virtue which is not subordinated to love of God. Milton loved music, and the devil 'suspended Hell' with their harmonies, but because their hearts were impure Hell soon reasserts itself. The devils do not 'lose all their virtue', but their remaining virtue is dross, worse than useless, because their wills are not subordinated to the will of God. Milton comes close to rejecting all Greek, all pagan, all non-Christian culture. He rejects all 'gay religions, full of pomp', preferring 'the upright heart and pure'. All virtue is in the heart and in the purity of the motive. Religion and politics in Milton's day were inseparable and he was opposed to what he thought of as the illegitimate authority of bishop and King. Like Satan, he was a rebel against what he thought of as tyranny, and no doubt this gave force to his presentation of Satan. He thought of bishop and King as assuming the authority which belonged rightfully to God. Like most people of his time he gave a higher value to the Old Testament than most people would be inclined to do today. It ought to be added, however, that Books I and II are grimmer and harsher than the poem as a whole; we haven't yet come to Adam and Eve in the Garden or the redemptive action of the Son.

Satan

We shall discuss Satan to a considerable extent in the commentary. Here, in summary are a few points to bear in mind:

1 Satan is a fallen angel. He was hurled from Heaven because 'he trusted to have equalled the Most High'; he refused to accept subordination to the Almighty and All-good.

2 He fell from a sense of 'injured merit' – a common and petty emotion. He is the incarnation of petty emotions – envy, spite, revenge – on a huge scale. The devils themselves physically change scale more than once; they are both pygmies and giants.

3 He yearns for Heaven, but suppresses the yearning. An important part of the Hell he lives in is the sense of deprivation.

4 He is the Father of Sin and Death, through which, since he can't be happy himself, he tries to make others as miserable as *he* is.

5 He is the Father of Lies. Like most of us when we lie, he doesn't always realize that he is lying.

6 He is a great orator, but uses oratory for his own purposes, without regard for truth.

7 He is a great leader, but where is he leading?

8 He has both energy and courage on an enormous scale. How valuable are these qualities *in themselves*? To what extent does it depend on the purpose for which they are used?

9 He claims that in Hell he is 'free'. What considerations about the meaning of the word 'freedom' does this suggest?

10 Satan is a skilled actor and showman. Are these abilities necessary to a successful leader?

11 Satan is seen as a dragon, as a leviathan, as a serpent. These incarnations are traditional – that is to say they have long had a hold on human imagination. Why?

12 How much 'sympathy' do we have with Satan? Do we sympathize with him for what he is in himself or because he is the most vividly drawn 'character' in the story? Why is it that the 'villain' of a story is nearly always more interesting than the 'hero'? Is it perhaps because Satan has succeeded all too well and rebellion against authority has become second nature to us?

13 Discussion of Satan rapidly turns into a series of questions. Most people have an ambiguous attitude towards him, feeling both attraction and repulsion. Many people, it is relevant to add, feel the same about snakes.

14 Is Milton's presentation of Satan big and forceful enough? If so, we have to look not to an analysis of his 'character' but to Milton's creation of him by poetic means.

Hell

We shall see how Milton makes Hell both a place and an internal state. Milton describes the physical Hell largely in traditional terms – darkness, fire, burning marl, sulphur, quicksands and so on. These images still have power to terrify, perhaps because they appeal to our subconscious and recur in dreams and nightmares. Moreover, they are the externals which correspond to the interior hell of hopelessness, violent conflicting passions, aggressive and insatiable egotism.

Many people, perhaps most people, no longer believe in Satan and in a physical Hell in any literal sense. Does this in any way spoil the poem, or does the myth still have power, and if so, why? What has the poem still to say about the moral condition of Man? It seems likely that the poem will appeal more to the unbeliever who responds to the vitality of the poetry than to the believer who does not.

Even believers, of course, will be faced with problems that are probably unanswerable. Does a merciful God really punish the wicked eternally in Hell? How did evil come into the world in the first place? Are we really 'free' and can human freedom be reconciled with God's Providence and Omniscience? Like the devils we soon become 'in wandering mazes lost'.

Summary of the complete poem

Ever since he was a boy Milton had been determined to write a great poem – great in subject-matter as well as in execution – which would rival, in his native tongue, the great epics of Latin, Greek and Italian. He felt that he was being led on to this by 'the will of Heaven' and with extraordinary steadiness of nerve and confidence in his destiny he devoted himself to study over many years until the time of 'inward ripeness' had arrived. In *Sonnet VII*, written probably in 1632, he had contemplated the swift passage of time and his continued unreadiness, and concluded:

> Yet be it less or more, or soon or slow,
>   It shall be still in strictest measure even
>   To that same lot, however mean or high,
> Towards which Time leads me, and the will of Heaven;
>   All is, if I have grace to use it so,
>   As ever in my great task-master's eye.

A quarter of a century passed before *Paradise Lost* was begun.

For a long time Milton was uncertain as to the subject-matter of his poem, even of the form it would take. In 1639 he was still thinking of writing about King Arthur. He once listed a hundred possible subjects, some from British history, some from the Bible. By 1640 he seems to have decided that his great work would be a dramatic tragedy on the Greek model. He made more than one draft of such a work on the subject, now, of Paradise lost, perhaps to be called 'Adam unparadiz'd'. Some lines of this tragedy were written and later incorporated into *Paradise Lost*. All these plans were abandoned while Milton involved himself in politics and polemics.

It may be helpful to give a brief summary of each of the twelve books of the poem, since it is important to see what part the first two Books play in the total structure.

Book I Satan and his followers are in Hell, following their expulsion from Heaven. Satan addresses his troops, reviving them. They may, he says, regain Heaven, or some new world. Pandemonium is built as a council-chamber.

Book II The devils debate their future. Beëlzebub proposes that they ruin God's new creation. Satan volunteers to undertake the task alone. He meets Sin and Death at the gates of Hell and voyages through Chaos.

Book III Heaven. God sees Satan coming and knows that he will succeed. The Son offers himself as Man's Redeemer. Meanwhile Satan finds his way to earth.

Book IV Satan comes to Eden, sees Adam and Eve, and overhears them discussing the Tree of Knowledge. He tries to tempt Eve in a dream, but is discovered by Gabriel, who has come to defend Man. Satan flies.

Book V Adam and Eve at worship and work. Raphael warns them of their danger and describes Satan's rebellion in Heaven.

Book VI Raphael describes the three days' war in Heaven and repeats his warning to Adam.

Book VII Raphael describes to Adam and Eve the creation of the world.

Book VIII Adam tells Raphael how he is forbidden to touch the Tree of Knowledge and describes the creation of Eve. Raphael departs.

Book IX Eve persuades Adam to allow her to go off and work on her own. Adam is reluctant, but agrees. Satan finds her alone and tempts her. She eats the fruit and persuades Adam to do the same.

Book X The Son descends to Eden and pronounces doom on Adam and Eve and the Serpent. Satan returns in triumph to Pandemonium. He, 'first in sin', will also be doomed. Sin and Death ascend to Eden, claiming the world as theirs. God foretells their overthrow by the Son. Through his Angels, God effects changes in the elements and the stars so that the Earth becomes susceptible to change and corruption. Adam and Eve repent and ask mercy of God.

Book XI God sends Michael to Eden to show the future to Adam, particularly his hope of Redemption. He shows him a vision of the world's history until the Flood.

Book XII Michael shows the world's history from the Flood to the coming of Christ, and the subsequent progress of Christianity. He leads Adam and Eve to the gates of Eden, from which they are gently expelled. They are assured of their ultimate salvation.

For convenience, the text of Books I and II has been divided up into sections comprising groups of lines, as follows:

Book I

1–26 Introduction and theme.
27–83 Satan's Fall from Heaven. Hell.
84–127 Satan to Beëlzebub.
128–55 Beëlzebub's reply.
156–270 Satan plans revenge.
271–330 Satan and Beëlzebub rouse the fallen angels.
331–621 The fallen angels.
622–798 Satan addresses his troops. The building of Pandemonium.

Book II

1–42 Satan opens the debate.
43–105 Moloch speaks.
106–228 Belial speaks.
229–83 Mammon speaks.
284–416 Beëlzebub proposes the master-plan.
417–505 Satan volunteers.
506–628 The devils disperse.
629–870 Satan's journey. He meets Sin and Death.
871–1055 Satan journeys through Chaos and Night until he is in sight of earth.

Book I: critical commentary, textual notes and revision questions

Lines 1–26 Introduction and theme

Milton's own account of the opening of his poem was as follows: 'This first book proposes first in brief the whole subject, man's first disobedience, and the loss thereupon of Paradise wherein he was placed; then touches the prime cause of his fall, the serpent, or rather Satan in the serpent, who revolting from God and drawing to his side many legions of angels was by the command of God driven out of Heaven with all his crew into the great deep.'

It is characteristic of Milton's mind that it ranges hugely backwards and forwards in time and space, and so it is in the span of opening lines: 'disobedience', 'death', 'woe', 'loss of Eden', 'one greater Man', 'regain the blissful seat' – the whole vast plan of his story is summed up. It is to be an 'adventurous song', of 'things unattempted yet in prose or rhyme'. To aid him he invokes the *'Heavenly Muse'*, the Holy Spirit which inspired Moses, the very Spirit which 'moved upon the face of the waters'. If the Holy Spirit created a structured universe out of 'the vast abyss', it can help him create order out of the chaos of his subject.

The second sentence comes home to the *purpose* of his poem – to 'assert Eternal Providence,/And justify the ways of God to men'. This is an ambition higher than that of his predecessors in the epic form: he intends to soar 'above the Aonian mount' and pursue 'Things unattempted yet in prose or rhyme'. The justification of God's ways was a favourite Miltonic theme: the Chorus in *Samson Agonistes* draws the conclusion that:

> All is best, though we oft doubt
> What the unsearchable dispose
> Of highest wisdom brings about.

Milton's own faith in God's justice must often have been tried. His political hopes had failed, and he was a blind, ageing man with little to show for a lifetime of study and endeavour. But both *Paradise Lost* and *Samson Agonistes* show how God brings good out of evil. Satan may appear to triumph by subverting Man, but God's reply – the Incarnation – is ready.

1 **Of Man's first disobedience** In the first six lines Milton, like Virgil and Homer before him, states his theme. There is an implied contrast with Virgil's 'Arma virumque cano' – 'Arms and the man I sing'.
  Fruit The word is a pun. Man's disobedience consisted in eating the fruit of the forbidden tree, but 'fruit' also means the *result* of the action, which 'brought death into the world and all our woe'.
2 **mortal** Bringing death.
4 **one greater Man** Christ, the 'second Adam'.
6 **Sing Heavenly Muse** The invocation of the Muse is in the epic convention. But Milton doesn't invoke one of the classical Muses: he invokes the *heavenly* Muse which inspired Moses.
7 **Oreb ... Sinai** Holy Mountains. Moses saw God in the burning bush on Oreb and took down the law from God on Sinai (Exodus, 19).
8 **That shepherd** Moses is supposed to have prefigured 'the good shepherd', Christ.
9 **In the beginning** The first words of Genesis.
11 **Siloa's brook** The classical Muses inhabited the spring and altar of Zeus. Milton adapts the idea by saying that the Heavenly Muse haunts the spring that flows by the Temple ('the oracle') of God.
12 **Fast by** Close by.
14 **no middle flight** Milton intends to rise to the highest Empyrean.
15 **the Aonian mount** Helicon, sacred to the classical Muses.
  pursues Treats of.
17 **O Spirit** The Holy Spirit. Milton believed that a great poem can be written only with the aid of the Holy Spirit.
18 **Before all temples the upright heart and pure** Milton, as a Protestant, emphasizes the importance of inner purity rather than external show.
19 **Thou from the first/Wast present** See the account of the creation in Genesis 1.
21 **the vast Abyss** Chaos.
24 **argument** Subject.
25 **assert** Vindicate.
  Eternal Providence God's plan for the world.

Lines 27–83 Satan's Fall from Heaven. Hell

Milton comes to his story. Why did Man fall, transgressing God's will 'For one restraint, lords of the world besides'?

Milton plunges straight into the middle of his story: the war in Heaven which resulted in Satan's fall is described later, in Books V and VI. The focus immediately falls on Satan, the biggest and most interesting character in the story, the hero – or anti-hero. He is presented, to begin with, in his lowest form as 'The infernal serpent', and his peculiar vices are listed – guile, envy, revenge, pride, ambition. Envy and revenge, in particular, are petty vices which Satan practises on a grand scale. His ambition is infinite – he 'trusted to have equalled the most High', an absurdly inflated, self-contradictory claim. He is engaged in a war which he can't ultimately win. There is emphasis on his pride and desire for self-glorification. There is a perverse grandeur about the lines:

> Against the throne and monarchy of God
> Raised impious war in Heaven and battle proud

but it collapses on 'With vain attempt' as though a trapdoor had been opened beneath him, and he continues throughout the poem to be both heroic and absurd, sometimes simultaneously, sometimes alternately. Inflation is always followed, sooner or later, by deflation.

The following headlong lines:

> Him the almighty Power
> Hurled headlong flaming from the ethereal sky
> With hideous ruin and combustion down
> To bottomless perdition

with their absence of punctuation, mime his dizzy fall from Heaven. Again the self-defeating nature of Satan's crime is emphasized: 'Who durst defy the Omnipotent to arms'.

Then we are given our first glimpse of Hell. Hell is seen in physical terms, of course, mostly of a traditional kind:

> A dungeon horrible, on all sides round
> As one great furnace flamed,

though Milton is careful not to be too particular and emphasizes the *negative* aspects of Hell: the flames give 'no light' and, in a strange paradox, the 'darkness' is 'visible'. But Hell is also a *mental* state. Satan is punished by:

> the thought
> Both of lost happiness and lasting pain.

He can still appreciate what he has chosen to lose, and he has to consume his sense of lost happiness in hatred lest it become unbearable. So, in Book IX, he is disarmed, on his first sight of Eve, by her beauty, but a few moments later 'the hot hell that always in him burns' overwhelms him. Hell is a place of spiritual deprivation:

> where peace
> And rest can never dwell, hope never comes.

The repeated 'never' is chilling. Satan carried Hell around with him. In Book IV he says 'My self am Hell'. Hell is being irrecoverably removed from God 'as from the centre thrice to the utmost pole'.

At the end of the section we are introduced to Satan's chief assistant, Beëlzebub. The name, coming as it does at the beginning of the line, explodes grotesquely, half horrific, half comic. The mixture is characteristic of Milton's presentation of the fallen angels.

29 **grand** First, original.
32 **For** Because of. Apart from the single prohibition that they are not to eat from the forbidden tree, Adam and Eve were 'lords of the world'.
36 **what time** At the time when.
39 **peers** Equals.
46 **ruin** Derived from the Latin 'ruina', meaning 'falling'.
   combustion Utter destruction; consumption by fire.
52 **gulf** Lake, whirlpool.
56 **baleful** Full of woe.
57 **witnessed** Showed, testified to.
64 **discover** Reveal.
66 **hope never comes** Milton was perhaps thinking of the famous words which, according to Dante, were written over the gates of Hell: 'Abandon hope, all you who enter here'.
68 **urges** Afflicts.
74 **As from the centre thrice to the utmost pole** The distance of Hell from the Empyrean is equal to three times the distance of the earth ('the centre') from the utmost pole of the universe.
78 **weltering** Rolling, wallowing.

81 **Beëlzebub** In the Bible, Beëlzebub is lord of the flies, the
   sun-god of the Philistines. In *Paradise Lost* he is next in
   rank to Satan.
82 **thence in Heaven called Satan** 'Satan' means 'adversary'.

Lines 84–127 Satan to Beëlzebub

This is a fine and revealing example of Satan's rhetoric, busy,
quick-moving and grandiloquent enough almost to conceal
the inner contradictions. There are the excuses for his failure:

> till then who knew
> The force of those dire arms?

to which the answer must presumably be 'Everybody', since
the Almighty must by definition be unbeatable in battle. He
manages to make 'He with his thunder' sound as though God
had taken unfair advantage by using an illegal weapon. He
never refers to God by name, but as 'He', 'the potent Victor',
'our grand Foe'. He makes a virtue out of his unwillingness to
'repent or change' – the very unwillingness which imprisons
him eternally in the hell of himself.

Much of what Satan says sounds grand and admirable
because of the rhetorical force with which it is expressed, but
when we look at it more closely it is seen to be hollow and even
absurd. He claims that in the war against God he 'shook His
throne' and that the battle was 'dubious', that it could have
gone either way. This is untrue. Satan is the Father of Lies.
The rhetoric of:

> What though the field be lost?
> All is not lost;

and the lines which follow, is superb, and much-imitated, in
good causes or ill, by war-leaders and politicians. The 'cour-
age never to submit or yield' may or may not be admirable; it
depends, perhaps, on the justice of the cause for which one is
fighting, and the motivating force behind Satan is the 'study of
revenge, immortal hate'.

What Satan will not do – cannot do – is 'bow and sue for
grace', and this refusal, no doubt, strikes an answering chord
of rebelliousness in ourselves. Perhaps it is impossible for

fallen man not to be, at least in part, on Satan's side. But Satan is refusing to bow to that which is, by definition, all-powerful and all-good. He refuses to acknowledge his own dependence. He likes to regard himself not as a created being but as self-created. He likes to pretend that Fate, not the will of God, rules the Universe. And he persuades himself that they may have learnt a lesson from defeat and, 'in foresight much advanced', will do better next time in the 'eternal war'.

Satan's brave face is, however, merely superficial. Beneath, he is 'racked with deep despair', his essential spiritual condition. His public face is that of the supreme dissembler, and it is impossible to know the extent to which he is deceived by his own rhetoric.

All rule, except his own, is 'tyranny' to Satan. He intends to set up a tyranny of his own in Hell.

98 **sense of injured merit** Satan rebelled through jealousy of the Son, who had been preferred to him. The 'sense of injured merit' is one of the pettiest of human emotions, though widespread.

104 **dubious** Doubtful in its outcome. The battle in Heaven lasted three days, but the outcome was never, in fact, doubtful.

109 **And what is else not to be overcome?** And what else is the meaning of not being overcome?

116 **by fate** Satan recognizes Fate, not God, as his superior. It was all, he implies, bad luck. He denies that the angels were created by God, claiming that they were self-created.

117 **this empyreal substance** Angels were thought to be made of a heavenly, flame-like substance which was indestructible and infinitely adaptable. Later, for instance, the devils shrink in size so as to squeeze into Pandemonium.

119 **in foresight much advanced** Satan claims that they have learnt by experience and will do better next time.

123 **triumphs** The word was accented on the second syllable.

Lines 128–55 Beëlzebub's reply

Beëlzebub, the born second-in-command, begins by flattering Satan and continues the myth that their rebellion had 'endangered' God. But the contradictions in their position soon emerge. Beëlzebub professes to be in doubt whether God's victory was achieved through 'strength, or chance, or fate', yet he must believe that 'our Conqueror' is 'almighty' since

> no less
> Than such could have o'erpowered such force as ours.

He also puts his finger on the tragic dilemma of the devils in Hell: that their 'heavenly essences' cannot perish, the 'mind and spirit remains/Invincible', but only so that they may be 'swallowed up in endless misery'. Following the logic of this he is a defeatist: their 'eternal being' serves only 'To undergo eternal punishment'.

128 **throned Powers** Angels. Throned is said as two syllables.
130 **conduct** Leadership.
134 **event** Result.
138 **Essences** Beings.
141 **extinct** Extinguished.
146 **entire** Whole.
148 **suffice** Satisfy.
150 **his business** The work God has appointed us to do.
152 **Deep** Chaos.
154 **being** Existence.

Lines 156–270 Satan plans revenge

Satan must scotch such defeatist talk. He replies with 'speedy words', clearly stating his destructive nihilism:

> To do aught good never will be our task,
> But ever to do ill our sole delight.

His aim is to 'pervert' God's providence, turning defeat into at least temporary victory, though he knows that God in his turn will convert evil to greater good. Indeed, Satan's ambition is heavily qualified: it 'oft-times *may* succeed, so as *perhaps*/Shall grieve him'. He knows in his heart that he is on a hiding to nothing and the worst he can do to God is cause Him temporary inconvenience. Still, it gives the devils something to do. They have need of incessant activity since to sit doing nothing is intolerable.

The landscape of Hell here is one of dreary emptiness, 'desolation, void of light', the physical equivalent of Satan's despair. Despair, because it denies or ignores the sovereign and redemptive power of God, is the ultimate vice, just as Hope is one of the theological virtues.

In the first of the poem's epic similes Satan is likened to a Leviathan (lines 200–9). Milton's similes have been criticized on the ground that they wander away and distract from the main point, and this particular simile has, perhaps, to modern ears, something inaptly comic about it even when we remember that in the seventeenth century highly exaggerated stories were current about the size of whales and other sea-monsters. It may also be said that the pilot who anchors his ship to a whale is deluded, living in a fool's paradise, and that Satan, the master illusionist, likes to make himself appear the friend of man until light dawns and the terror of the situation is revealed. At any rate, the simile returns to Satan with violent effect in the grotesquely ugly and elongated 'So stretched out huge in length the arch-fiend lay' (line 209).

When Satan speaks again it is at first with an impassioned sense of home-sickness and loss. He knows that he has exchanged 'this mournful gloom' for 'that celestial light', but he can't allow himself to think of this bad bargain for more than a second. He again drowns misery in impassioned rhetoric and the assertion of his own ego and will. He says he has a 'mind not to be changed by place or time' – though he is always changing: true consistency is impossible to him. He thinks that he can 'make a heaven of hell, a hell of heaven', since 'The mind is its own place'; and this is true, since Heaven, which required subordination and obedience, to him was Hell, and he will carry Hell with him wherever he goes. At least in Hell he will be boss, and he thinks it 'Better to reign in Hell, than serve in Heaven'. It is a characteristically Satanic device to turn 'serve' into a dirty word. He will, he says, be 'free', free to be himself; rigid, fixed in his own ego, itself a definition of Hell.

158 **Doing or suffering** Whether we are active or passive.
167 **if I fail not** If I am not mistaken.
168 **counsels** Plans.
172 **laid** Stilled, laid to rest.
178 **slip** Let slip.
186 **afflicted powers** Routed forces.

196 **rood** A measure of length, as in 'rod, pole or perch'. About 5 metres (5½ yards).

197 **As whom** As those whom.
   fables The classical myths. Milton speaks of them disparagingly as 'fabulous'.

198 **Titanian, or Earth-born** The Titans were giant off-spring of Uranus and Ge (the earth).

199 **Briareos or Typhon** Serpentine monsters. Typhon was hundred-headed. He tried to seize sovereignty over gods and men but was vanquished by Zeus with a thunderbolt and buried under Etna.

200 **Tarsus** The capital of Cilicia, Typhon's home.

201 **Leviathan** The whale, or other sea-monster.

204 **night-foundered** Benighted.

205 **Deeming some island** Some highly-coloured tales about the size of whales were clearly current in the seventeenth century.

207 **the lee** The sheltered side.

208 **Invests** Wraps.

226 **incumbent** Leaning.

230 **as when the force/Of subterranean wind** Earthquakes were thought to be caused by the escape of underground winds.

232 **Pelorus** Near Etna.

236 **bottom** Crater.
   involved Wrapped in.

239 **Stygian** Of Hell. The Styx flowed round Tartarus.

241 **Supernal** Heavenly.

244 **change** Take in exchange for.

246 **dispose and bid** Arrange and command.

248 **Whom reason hath equalled, force hath made supreme** Satan claims that they were God's equal in reason though not in power.

257 **all but less than** Nearly equal to.

266 **astonished** Thunderstuck.
   oblivious Bringing unconsciousness.

268 **mansion** Place.

Lines 271–330 Satan and Beëlzebub rouse the fallen angels

Satan, supported by his vast spear, crosses the 'burning lake' to where his angels (hereinafter known as devils) 'lay entranced'. The pain of the journey and the courage required to make it are a small intimation of the greater, even more perilous, journey he is shortly to take.

Of the famous simile of the leaves of Vallombrosa, C.

Falconer commented in his *Essay on Milton's Imitations of the Ancients*, (1741): 'it not only expresses a multitude ... but also the posture and situation of the angels. Their lying confusedly in heaps, covered with the Lake, is finely represented by this image of the leaves in the brooks. Moreover, the falling of a shower of leaves from the trees in a storm of wind very well represents the ejection of the angels from their former celestrial mansions; and "their faded splendor wan" (Book IV, line 870) is finely expressed by the paleness and witheredness of the leaves'.

Dead leaves are an ancient symbol of the dead. Then Milton shifts the simile to compare the devils with Pharaoh's army overwhelmed by the Red Sea. By comparison with his 'abject' (in both the old and the modern senses of the word) host, Satan seems indeed a hero.

He rouses his followers by the crude use of sarcasm, as well as a fear-inspiring warning that, if they just lie there, God will take the chance to 'Transfix us to the bottom of this gulf'.

274 **pledge** Assurance.
276 **edge** Front line.
281 **amazed** Utterly confounded.
282 **pernicious** Destructive.
285 **Ethereal temper** Made in Heaven.
288 **optic glass** Telescope.
  the Tuscan artist Galileo. Milton had visited Galileo in Italy.
289 **Fesole** A hill about five kilometres (three miles) from Florence, where Galileo lived.
290 **Valdarno** In the valley of the river Arno.
291 **her spotty globe** Galileo had described the uneven surface of the moon.
294 **ammiral** Flagship.
296 **marl** Soil.
299 **Nathless** Nevertheless.
302 **Thick as autumnal leaves** Dead leaves were a common image for the dead.
303 **Vallombrosa** 'Shady valley', full of trees, about thirty kilometres (eighteen miles) from Florence.
  Etrurian Tuscan.
304 **sedge** The Red Sea was known as the 'Sea of Sedge' because of the amount of seaweed in it.
305 **when with fierce winds Orion armed** The constellation of Orion was accompanied at its rising and setting by fierce storms. Orion is shown as having a sword and club.

306 **vexed** Violently disturbed.
307 **Busiris** Wrongly supposed by Milton to be the Pharaoh who
   perished in the Red Sea. For the story see Exodus 14.
   Memphian chivalry Egyptian forces. Memphis was the
   ancient capital of Egypt. 'Chivalry' is presumably sarcastic.
308 **perfidious** Treacherous, because he had given the Israelites
   leave to go.
309 **the sojourners of Goshen** The Israelites were held in
   captivity in Goshen.
312 **Abject** Cast down.
318 **or have ye chosen this place** The passage, of course, is
   heavily sarcastic.
320 **virtue** Valour.

Revision questions on lines 1–330

1 Examine Beëlzebub's reply to Satan (lines 128–55)
showing what it reveals of his character and his relationship
to Satan.

2 What features of Hell does Milton focus on, through
direct description and dialogue, in this opening section of
Paradise Lost? How far does he succeed here in giving
concrete form to a place which is, by definition, almost
beyond description or imagination?

Lines 331–621 The Fallen Angels

This is the most difficult passage in the first two books for the
modern reader to come to grips with. The profusion of neces-
sary notes tells its story. Milton and his readers were more
familiar than most of us are today with the Old Testament,
particularly the books of Kings and Chronicles. It is import-
ant in reading the passage not to get bogged down in notes;
read it freely, preferably aloud, and much of its force will come
through; but for a fuller understanding we need to follow
Milton's range of reference.

First, the devils are likened to the locusts which Moses
called down as a plague on Egypt. Locusts were a common
metaphor for devils, and insects may still be used, particularly
en masse or in a 'pitchy cloud', as an image of evil, e.g. in a
horror movie. Later in the same paragraph (line 353) the

devils are compared to the barbarian hordes who attacked Rome in the fourth and fifth centuries AD. They are the innumerable enemies of civilization – Vandals with and without the capital letter.

In the following extended passage we see the devils as pagan gods. It was the orthodoxy of the time that they 'Got them new names', under which names they were worshipped by the other, pagan, non-Judaic religions. In the Old Testament Yaweh was a jealous god, the only true God, who would not tolerate the worship of any god other than Himself. The Israelites were frequently guilty of being seduced by the false gods of neighbouring tribes, gods which often took animal form – 'the image of a brute'; or they were 'gay religions full of pomp and gold' (line 372). This last phrase reminds us that Milton also had, in the front of his mind, the Reformation, which had, in the Protestant view, suppressed Catholic idolatry. Milton, moreover, regarded the gods and goddesses of Greece and Rome as idols, superior to the brute Egyptian gods, no doubt, but idols nevertheless. 'The Lord thy God is one God.'

There follows, then, a parade of the pagan gods – 'abominations'. First Moloch, 'besmeared with blood of human sacrifice', whom the Ammonites worshipped as a sun-god. Children were burnt as a sacrifice to him, and Solomon worshipped him. Then Chemos, whose worship involved 'lustful orgies' and ritual copulation. So we have 'lust hard by hate'. Some of the pagan gods are described with lyrical, pastoral, alluring grace, like Astarte:

> To whose bright image nightly by the moon
> Sidonian virgins paid their vows and songs

But Milton intends the allurement to be specious, like the attraction of Satan, disguised as the serpent, when he deceives Eve.

Crude violence is never very far away, the penalty of departing from the one true God. Dagon is pictured, '... head and hands lopped off/In his own temple on the grunsel edge', followed by the animal gods of Egypt, and Belial, who filled 'With lust and violence the house of God', and was responsible for the homosexuality, male and female, practised by Israel's neighbouring tribes. Such are the horrors and

delusions to which the devils have deceived mankind through-
out history.

Showing 'semblance of worth, not substance', Satan soon
rouses his troops from despair to order, discipline, 'perfect
phalanx', though they are only in the *guise* of 'warriors old'.
Satan is now a military commander. His heart 'distends with
pride' at the sight of his troops and, with a weight of emphasis
which makes it almost ridiculous, 'glories'. All the great
armies of the past, and of past epics, are compared unfavour-
ably with the greatness of this army. The descriptions of the
armies of chivalry – 'When Charlemagne with all his peerage
fell/By Fontarabbia' is impressive and beautiful, but it also
speaks of a time when Christian chivalry was defeated by
pagan armies.

Satan addresses himself to the task of raising his legions
from their torpor. We are reminded that he is indeed an
Archangel, though 'ruined'. His courage is 'dauntless',
however misplaced, for the greatest evil is done with the
greatest courage. He even feels momentarily 'remorse and
passion to behold/The fellows of his crime'. Their glory is
withered, like great trees blasted by lightning. But he soon
puts such sentimentality behind him.

332 **wont** Accustomed.
339 **Amram's son** Moses.
341 **warping** Undulating.
345 **cope** Roof.
348 **Sultan** Used generally of tyrants.
351 **like which the populous North** These lines refer to the
    invasion of Italy and the Roman Empire by the Goths.
353 **Rhene or the Danaw** The Rhine or the Danube.
355 **Beneath** South of.
365 **Got them new names** Milton adopts the view that the fallen
    angels became the gods of heathenism, and in the passage
    which follows Milton uses these 'new names'.
366 **high sufferance** Over-ruling permission.
372 **gay religions full of pomp and gold** Milton often
    expresses his contempt for rich ceremony and ritual.
373 **for** As if they were.
380 **promiscuous** Confused in their ranks, disordered.
382 **durst fix/Their seats, long after, next the seat of
    God** Milton begins with those who led astray the Israelites,
    the chosen people.

386 **throned/Between the Cherubim** Altars to pagan gods were
set up inside the temple itself – see 2 Kings 21. The
cherubim were the gold figures at each end of the ark in the
Temple's Holy of Holies.

389 **Abominations** The Biblical word of idolatry.

392 **Moloch** The god of the sun, 'the abomination of the children
of Ammon' in 1 Kings, 11. According to 2 Kings, 23 he was
worshipped with human sacrifices, particularly of children.

394 **timbrels** Tambourines.

397 **Rabba ... Argob ... Ba san ... Arnon** Places occupied by
the Ammonites.

400 **neighbourhood** Nearness.

401 **Solomon** Solomon was wise, yet he had 700 wives and 300
concubines, many of them foreign, who persuaded him to
worship their Gods.
by fraud By deceit.

402 **His temple** The temple of Moloch.

403 **On that opprobious hill** The Mount of Olives, where
Solomon built altars to Moloch. So it became known as 'the
mount of corruption'.

404 **The pleasant valley of Hinnom** This was the scene of the
rites paid to Moloch and became the refuse-place of
Jerusalem. Fires were kept burning there, hence 'Tophet', a
name for Hell.

405 **Gehenna** Another name for Hell.

406 **Chemos** The idol of the Moabites.

407 **Aroer** This and the places which follow were in the land of
the Moabites.

411 **the Asphaltic Pool** The Dead Sea.

413 **Israel in Sittim** The nomadic Israelites had lived in a part
of Moab called Sittim. There they worshipped Peor.

414 **To do him wanton rites** The worship of Peor involved
ritual copulation with local women.
which cost them woe The leaders were killed on Moses'
orders and they were visited by plague.

415 **Yet thence his lustful orgies he enlarged** Later, the rites
were introduced to Jerusalem by Solomon, who worshipped
Peor as well as Moloch. 'Orgies' simply means 'rites'.
'Enlarged' means 'spread further'.

418 **good Josiah** King Josiah reformed Jerusalem and turned the
valley of Hinnom into a rubbish dump.

422 **Baalim and Ashtaroth** The supreme male deity of the
Phoenicians and Canaanites was Baal. He was worshipped
locally under different titles – e.g. Baal-Zebub, lord of the
flies – and the collective name for these manifestations of the
god was Baalim. Similarly, Ashtaroth was the collective
name for the moon-goddess Ashtareth, Baal's female
counterpart.

424 **Can either sex assume** cf. Pope, in the *Rape of the Lock*:
'For spirits, freed from mortal laws, with ease Assume what sexes and what shape they please.'

429 **Dilated** Expanded.

433 **Their Living Strength** Yahweh, 'the living God'.

439 **with crescent horns** The moon-goddess was represented as horned, like the crescent moon.

441 **Sidonian virgins** Sidon was the capital of Phoenicia.

446 **Thammuz** The God of the sun and fertility, the equivalent of the Greek Adonis.

447 **Whose annual wound in Lebanon** In legend, Thammuz was slain by a wild boar in Lebanon. His death and rising again were celebrated annually, corresponding with the seasons.

448 **The Syrian damsels to lament his fate** Thammuz's death was lamented when plants died in the heat of summer.

450 **While smooth Adonis** The river Adonis ran with red mud in spring.

455 **Ezekiel saw** See Ezekiel 14.

457 **Next came one** Dagon, the corn-god and the fish-god of the Philistines.

458 **when the captive ark** The Philistines captured the ark from the Israelites and took it to Dagon's temple. In the morning, 'Behold Dagon was fallen upon his face to the ground before the ark of the Lord; and the head of Dagon and both the palms of his hands were cut off upon the threshold'.
(I Samuel, 5.)

460 **grunsel** Threshold.

464 **Azotus** Here and in the following lines Milton names the five principal Philistine cities.

467 **Rimmon** The Syrian sky-god of Damascus. Syria lay between the rivers Abbana and Pharpha.

471 **A leper once he lost** Naaman, a Syrian captain, was cured of leprosy by Elisha, who persuaded him to wash in the Jordan.
and gained a king King Ahaz of Judah plundered the Temple to pay for help in a war against Syria. He defeated Syria and Ahaz replaced the temple altar by a copy of Rimmon's altar. (2 Kings, 16)

472 **sottish** Foolish.

478 **Osiris, Isis, Orus** Egyptian gods had animal heads or appeared in the form of animals. Osiris, the god of the dead, was worshipped under the form of a bull; Isis, goddess of the earth and fertility, had the body of a woman and the head of a cow; Orus (Horus), the god of day, was a hawk.

479 **abused** Deluded.

484 **The calf in Oreb** The Israelites' worship of the golden calf in the wilderness is described in Exodus, 32.

the rebel king Jeroboam, who opposed Solomon's son, Rehoboam.

485 **Doubled that sin** Jeroboam made *two* golden calves, one in Bethel, the other in Dan. He told the Israelites that the golden calves were the gods who had brought them out of Egypt, thus identifying 'his Maker', Jehovah, with the 'grass-fed ox'; but Jehovah had killed 'all the first-born in the land of Egypt ... and all the first-born of cattle'. (Exodus, 12)

489 **bleating** The Egyptian deity, Ammon, was worshipped in the form of a ram.

490 **Belial** Belial wasn't a god (hence 'no temple stood/Or altar smoked') but an abstract term meaning 'that which is without profit' or worthlessness. Milton makes Belial the type of unnatural vice and lust – found in the 'house of God' and in 'courts and palaces'.

495 **Eli's sons** The sons of the high priest, Eli, desecrated the temple by sleeping with its maidservants. Milton may perhaps have been thinking of some seventeenth century priests.

501 **the sons/Of Belial, flown with insolence and wine** Milton was probably thinking of the seventeenth century street-bullies or 'muggers' who attacked people by night in the streets of London.

502 **flown** Flushed.

503 **the streets of Sodom** Two angels visited Lot in Sodom. Sodomite homosexuals tried to rape them, though Lot offered them his daughters. See Genesis, 19.

504 **Gibeah** Judges, 19 tells the story of a man whose concubine ran away. He fetched her back and stayed in Gibeah with a kindly old man. The local homosexuals (referred to as 'the sons of Belial') again wanted the man, but he offered them his concubine and they raped her to death.

508 **Ionian** Greek.
of Javan's issue held/Gods Christians believed that the Greeks were descended from Javan, Noah's grandson.

509 **yet confessed later than Heaven and Earth/Their boasted parents** 'Confessed later' means 'admitted to be of later origin'. The Greeks believed that their ancestors were gods descended from Uranus and Ge (Heaven and Earth). Milton is trying to prove that the Greeks were a subsequent development of the Hebrew line and their gods therefore inferior to the Christian god.

510 **Titan, Heaven's first-born** The twelve sons of Uranus and Ge were called Titans. Milton refers to the eldest as 'Titan'. A younger son, Saturn, deposed his elder brother, and he, in turn, was deposed by Jove, whose mother was Rhea. Thus Jove, some distance removed from Uranus, and Ge, was a usurper.

511 **enormous** Monstrous.

514 **Crete** Jove was born in Crete, on Mount Ida.

516 **Olympus** The mountain range in northern Greece, home of the Greek gods.
ruled the middle air/Their highest heaven This is contemptuous: it wasn't *very* high.

517 **the Delphian cliff,/Or in Dodona** There were oracles at Delphi and Dodona.

519 **Doric land** Greece.
Saturn old/Fled over Adria to the Hesperian fields Saturn is said to have crossed the Adriatic and spread the Greek religion in Italy ('the Hesperian fields').

521 **o'er the Celtic** i.e. the Celtic fields – France and perhaps Spain.
the utmost Isles Britain.

523 **damp** Depressed.

526 **his** Satan's.

528 **recollecting** Gathering together again.

536 **advanced** Lifted up.

538 **emblazed** Emblazoned – a heraldic term.

541 **universal** Entire.

542 **Hell's concave** Hell's vaulted roof.

543 **reign** Realm.

546 **orient** Bright.

548 **serried** Close-set.

549 **Anon.** Immediately.

550 **perfect phalanx** A phalanx was a solid formation used by the Spartans (Dorians).
the Dorian mood/Of flutes Plato called the Dorian mode in music 'the mode of courage'. The Spartans went into battle to the music of flutes.

554 **Deliberate** Controlled.

556 **suage** Assuage.

563 **Advanced in view** In ranks, ready to be reviewed.
horrid lit. 'bristling'. Here, perhaps, bristling with spears.

568 **traverse** From side to side.

573 **since created Man** Since the creation of man.

575 **that small infantry/Warred on by cranes** The pygmies. Milton is saying that all the great armies of the past, in legend and history, were pygmies compared with Satan's army.

577 **Phlegra** Where the giants who fought the Olympian gods were born.

578 **Ilium** Troy.

579 **Mixed with auxiliar gods** Gods assisted either side.

580 **Uther's son** King Arthur.

581 **Begirt with** Surrounded by.
Armoric From Brittany.

582 **all who since** The Crusaders, and those whom they fought against.

585 **Or whom Biserta sent** The Arabs from Bizerta against whom Charlemagne and the French knights fought.

587 **Thus far these beyond** Even though they were so far beyond comparison with any mortal warriors, they still obeyed ('observed') Satan.

597 **eclipse** An eclipse was thought to be an evil omen, particularly of a change of King. Charles II's censor objected to these lines.
disastrous The word still had astrological overtones – 'boding calamity'.

601 **intrenched** Cut into.

603 **considerate** Considering, thoughtful.

605 **remorse** Pity.

606 **fellows of** Companions in.

609 **amerced** Deprived of.

611 **For his revolt** Because of Satan's revolt.
yet faithful how they stood Yet he grieved to see how faithfully they stood.

613 **scathed** Singed.

Lines 622–798 Satan addresses his troops. The building of Pandemonium

Again Satan, who manages to be both repetitive and inconsistent, makes excuses for failing to win the war in Heaven. This time he manages to lay the blame for his revolt on God, who concealed his strength, 'Which tempted our attempt and wrought our fall.' An extraordinary story! Now that they know God's strength they could try again, but they would be advised this time to trust to 'fraud or guile'. Already there is rumour of a new world, inhabited by 'a generation . . . equal to the sons of Heaven' . They could go there, 'if but to pry', and if this suggestion makes them sound too much like Peeping Toms or petty burglars, he drowns it in another dose of rhetoric:

> For who can think submission? War, then war,
> Open or understood, must be resolved.

The double 'r' in the original spelling 'Warr' gave the word a robuster ring than it has today. To make war by prying is a supreme example of having it both ways. Satan uses words merely for effect.

The troops answer with a tremendous salute from 'millions

of flaming swords'. They make a great din, 'Hurling defiance towards the vault of Heaven', but the noise is empty clamour, a grand, easy gesture which costs nothing. The flame from their swords may 'illumine Hell', but that's a doubtful pleasure: even the devils' moment of apparent triumph only gives them a better view of their own degradation.

At last the devils have something to do. Led by Mammon they dash to the site of what is to be Pandemonium. Mammon is cartooned, as though in a morality play, as a crook-back, one whose 'looks and thoughts were always downward bent': even in Heaven it was the golden pavements he admired, not the 'vision beatific'. Milton pours scorn on the rape of the earth for gold and sees the building of the pyramids and the Tower of Babel as monuments only to the devilish pride of man, though there follows some admiration for the technological skill which goes into the building.

The architect is Mulciber – the Roman Vulcan or the Greek Hephaestus. In legend he had built the palaces of the gods on Olympus until he was thrown out by Jove. Milton describes how 'his hand was known/In heaven by many a towered structure high', residences for 'sceptred angels', 'Each in his hierarchy, the orders bright'. There is a spectacular description of Mulciber's fall, prefiguring the fall of Satan:

> from morn
> To noon he fell, from noon to dewy eve
> A summer's day,

where the swing-over of 'from morn/To noon' – an unusual place to have a line-break – captures the sensation of leaving your stomach behind in a rapidly descending lift. Milton's disconcertingly harsh morality is evident in the grim 'nor aught availed him now/To have built in Heaven high towers', and his contempt for mere art, skill or science when it isn't used with purity of heart and intention is apparent in 'headlong sent/With his industrious crew to build in hell'.

The name Pandemonium – which is Milton's invention – has that mixture of grandiloquence and absurdity characteristic of Hell. Soon, in an onomatopoeic passage, the devils are likened to bees, buzzing, busy, expectant. The devils reduce themselves to 'less than smallest dwarfs' to fit into the 'hall/Of that infernal court'; the reduction in size is also a comment on their essential pettiness. By contrast, their leaders retain their own dimensions and 'In close recess and secret conclave sat'. The idea that 'the great consult' exists for democratic discussion is largely pretence. The Praesidium has already met and what follows is, at least in part, a staged, dummy debate.

624 **event** Result.
632 **puissant** Powerful.
635 **For me, be witness** As for me, I swear before all the host of heaven that our defeat was not my fault. I didn't run away from danger or fail to take advice.
644 **So as not either to provoke** We know God's strength and our own. So we won't provoke him; but if he provokes us we won't dread him.
651 **fame** Report, rumour.
656 **eruption** Escape from Hell.
662 **understood** Understood among ourselves and so secret.
663 **out-flew/Millions of flaming swords** This was how Roman soldiers greeted a general's speech.
666 **Highly** With drunken arrogance. Compare the modern colloquial 'high'.
673 **That in his womb was hid** In Milton's day mining was regarded as rape of Mother Earth.
676 **pioneers** Those employed by the army to prepare the way for them, e.g. by digging trenches.
678 **cast** Form by throwing up the earth.
    Mammon An abstract word, like Belial, meaning 'wealth'.
679 **least erected** Lowest, least rational.
685 **suggestion** Temptation, subversion.
686 **the centre** The centre of the earth.
690 **ribs** Bars, large pieces.
    admire Wonder.
692 **bane** Source or cause of evil.
694 **Memphian** Egyptian. The Tower of Babel and the Pyramids are seen as signs of human pride.
702 **Sluiced** Led by sluices.
703 **founded** Melted.
704 **Severing** Separating.
    bullion-dross The scum rising from the bullion – separating the impurities.
706 **various** Complex.
707 **strange** Ingenious.
710 **Anon** Presently, soon.
711 **exhalation** Escape of gas.
712 **symphonies** Harmonious sounds.

713 **pilasters** Square columns.
   round In a circle.
715 **architrave** The master-beam that rests on a row of
   pillars.
716 **bossy sculptures** Sculptures in relief.
717 **fretted gold** Gold with patterns on it.
718 **Alcairo** Memphis, capital of Egypt.
720 **Belus** Baal, a Babylonian god.
   Serapis An Egyptian god.
722 **pile** Building.
723 **Stood fixed her stately height** Having reached its
   appointed height was now finished.
724 **discover** Reveal.
728 **cressets** A hanging lamp consisting of lumps of asphalt in
   baskets, fed with naphtha.
737 **hierarchy** There were nine orders of angels.
738 **his name** i.e. the architect's.
739 **Ausonian** Italian. The Roman Mulciber was the god of fire
   and metalsmiths, architect of the Olympian palaces of the
   gods. Zeus threw him out following an argument in Heaven
   in which Mulciber (Vulcan) took Juno's side against Jove.
750 **engines** Inventions, contrivances.
751 **industrious** Working in industry.
756 **Pandemonium** 'The home of all the demons.' Milton coined
   the word.
759 **By place or choice the worthiest** The best were appointed
   or elected.
763 **Though like a covered field** i.e. Pandemonium was full
   although it was as big as a roofed field such as was used for
   tournaments.
   champions Combatants.
764 **Soldan's** Sultan's.
765 **Paynim** Pagan.
766 **career** Gallop at the enemy; an attempt to unseat him with
   the lance.
769 **when the Sun with Taurus rides** Taurus, the bull, is one
   of the signs of the Zodiac, 19 April–20 May. So the time was
   spring.
774 **New rubbed with balm** The entrances to bee-hives were
   rubbed with herbs to attract the bees.
   expatiate Walk about.
776 **straitened** Crowded together.
779 **Now less than smallest dwarfs** Spirits could change their
   shape and size.
781 **the Indian mount** The Himalayas. Pygmies, about ·46m (18
   in.) high, were thought to live beyond the Himalayas.
785 **arbitress** Witness.
790 **were at large** i.e. they had plenty of room to move about.

795 **close recess** Secret retirement.
797 **Frequent** Crowded.
798 **consult** Debate. Here used as a noun.

Revision questions on lines 331–798

1 What qualities of leadership does Satan display in the second half of Book I?

2 What does the last section of Book I (from line 670 onwards) tell us about Milton's attitude towards wealth and materialism?

Book II: critical commentary, textual notes and revision questions

Lines 1—42 Satan opens the debate

The curtain goes up. Satan, the great showman, is discovered 'High on a throne of royal state', glittering with the wealth and splendour of the East. The word that carries most emphasis is 'barbaric', associated with tyranny, luxury, cruelty. Satan is referred to elsewhere as 'Sultan'. The first sentence comes to its climax on 'Satan exalted sat' – a phrase which is like a hiss. The contradiction in Satan's situation is well expressed in the paradox of 'by merit raised/To that bad eminence': Satan deserves his position as chief of Hell.

Satan begins as usual with flattery. The devils are 'Powers and Dominions', which also bolsters his own self-esteem as their overlord. His language has an apparent, though empty, dignity. He boosts morale by asserting that they are stronger by their fall. They will, he says again, have learnt by experience, though Milton, only a few lines earlier, had told us that Satan was 'by success untaught'.

Next, he justifies his position as leader. The great emphasis on the first word, 'Me', is significant. Anticipating possible rivalry, he claims leadership by right of seniority, election and merit. Moreover, he claims that he is safer than God in Heaven: God's subordinates may well envy Him – Satan judges others by himself – but nobody will envy Satan, who is most exposed to 'the Thunderer's aim' and condemned to 'greatest share of endless pain'. Satan, still adept at having it both ways, says that nobody would want *his* job; he is being unselfish, he implies, by accepting it.

He throws the meeting open to phony debate. Shall there be 'open war or covert guile'? He has already, in fact, devised his own plan which Beëlzebub will reveal when the moment is ripe.

2 **Ormus** An island in the Persian gulf, famous for pearls and jewels.
3 **Or where** Or of the places where.

4 **Showers on her kings** Oriental kings were showered with gold-dust at their coronation.

5 **by merit raised** It's a doubtful compliment to say that Satan *deserved* the throne of Hell.

9 **success** Events.

14 **I give not Heaven for lost** I do not consider heaven as lost.

17 **And trust themselves** Have such confidence in themselves that they won't fear that they will be beaten again.

18 **Me though just right** Satan asserts his right to the throne of Hell because of his seniority in Heaven, his election by the 'free choice' of the devils, his achievements in counsel and in war, and his raising them from the lake of fire.

23 **unenvied** Unenviable.

24 **state** Constitution, which in Heaven is based on rank.

28 **the Thunderer's** God's.

39 **Surer to prosper** i.e. things are so bad that they can only improve.

Lines 43–105 Moloch speaks

The first speaker is Moloch, a parody of a particular kind of bluff, unthinking military mind. 'My sentence is for open war'. It's as simple as that: he plunges straight in, without introduction or subtlety. He has no time for 'wiles', for planning, even for thought. He recognizes that Hell is 'a dark opprobrious den of shame', he wants to get out of it, and he has millions of men to hurl over the top and do the job. As he describes those who 'sit lingering here', his syntax becomes roundabout, mocking. Carried away by his almost hysterical belligerence he envisages 'Black fire and horror shot with equal rage/Among the angels'. He pours scorn on those who fear 'the event' – i.e. those who fear they might lose: after all, what can God do to them which he hasn't done already? The worst that can happen is that they will be obliterated entirely, which would be 'happier far/Than miserable to have eternal being'. Even Moloch can hardly pretend that they would have any real chance of *winning* the war; they might, however, disturb God's throne, which, he concludes with ringing absurdity, 'if not Victory is yet Revenge'. He advocates beating his head against the wall in the hope that the wall may suffer a dent.

43 **Moloch** He had been conspicuous in the battle in Heaven.

50 **thereafter** Accordingly.

51 **sentence** Opinion, vote.
52 **more unexpert** i.e. he is less experienced in wiles than in war.
58 **opprobious** Disgraceful.
59 **The prison of his tyranny** The prison assigned by God's tyranny.
63 **our tortures** The things that torture us.
65 **engine** The chariot of wrath that expelled them from Heaven.
69 **Tartarean** Tartarus was the Greek name for the underworld.
   strange fire The fire of Hell was different in kind from the fire of Heaven.
73 **Let such bethink them** Let such as think the way difficult remember.
75 **in our proper motion we ascend** It is natural to us, as spirits, to rise.
77 **Who but felt** Who did not feel?
79 **Insulting** Assaulting.
82 **event** Outcome. What follows anticipates a possible objection.
83 **Our stronger** God.
89 **exercise** Torment.
94 **what doubt we** Why do we hesitate?
97 **essential** The essence, substance, of their angelic forms.
   happier far/Than miserable to have eternal being It is better to be annihilated than to live for ever in misery.
101 **On this side nothing** We have already reached the worst, short of being absolutely annihilated.
   proof Experience.
104 **fatal** Secure because upheld by Fate.

Lines 106–228 Belial speaks

Belial is a good deal more intelligent than Moloch, which isn't difficult. He is suave, orderly, up to a point rational; all smooth surface, but inside 'false and hollow'. He uses the rhetorical device of asking loaded questions and answering them himself, piling them one on top of another – 'What if . . . what if?' He sees that to make war against God is pointless. He rightly points out that Moloch 'grounds his courage on despair' and questions Moloch's notion of revenge. They couldn't, he argues, take God by surprise (though Moloch would scorn anything as subtle as surprise), nor could they break their way in by force. They are better off as they are, not tempting the Almighty to obliterate them:

> for who would lose,
> Though full of pain, this intellectual being,

After all, he argues, things aren't so bad:

> Is this then worst,
> Thus sitting, thus consulting, thus in arms?

Belial, one feels, can't be too unhappy as long as he is able to show his intellectual superiority to Moloch. Things were a lot worse when they were driven from Heaven. With cool skill he winds through the rhetorical questions, piling up pictures of the infinitely worse things that might happen to them, binding the argument together with 'Is this then worst?' ... 'that sure was worse' ... 'this would be worse'. In time, he says, they will acclimatize themselves to Hell, and if they lie doggo 'Our supreme Foe in time may much remit/His anger' and perhaps 'Not mind us not offending' – the negatives are significant of his attitude.

Milton's comment on Belial is curtly dismissive:

> Thus Belial with words clothed in reasons' garb
> Counselled ignoble ease, and peaceful sloth,
> Not peace.

Milton had a particular contempt for 'peaceful sloth' and the attitude of mind which is too quietist to take action and can make an easy chair out of Hell itself.

106 **denounced** Proclaimed.
109 **Belial** 'Wicked counsellor'. He is presented as good-looking and persuasive.
111 **dignity** Honour.
113 **manna** Honey.
120 **urged/Main reason** Urged as the main reason for.
123 **success** Result, whether good or bad.
124 **fact** Deeds, feats.
132 **obscure** Dark.
134 **Or could we** Even if we could.
139 **the ethereal mould/Incapable of stain** The fiery substance of God and the angels in Heaven would soon prevail over the baser fire of Hell.
147 **intellectual being** Mental life.
149 **rather** Instead.
151 **sense** Sensation.
152 **Let this be good** Even if, for the sake of argument, we admit that it would be good to be annihilated.

156 **Belike through impotence** No doubt through lack of self-restraint. Said sarcastically.

165 **What when** How was it when?
amain With all speed.

175 **firmament** Roof.

182 **racking** Driving along. Perhaps torturing.

186 **hopeless end** With no end to hope for.

191 **motions** Schemes.

194 **Shall we, then, live thus vile** Shall we go on living in our present vile state? Belial proposes an objection to his argument which he then demolishes.

199 **To suffer, as to do,/Our strength is equal** The syntax of this sentence is obscure, but what Belial is saying is that they have as much strength to endure as they have to attack, and they must have known this when they took the offensive against so great an enemy.

212 **Not mind us not offending** Forget about us if we don't offend him.

216 **or, inured not feel** Or not feel them, having become accustomed to them.

218 **temper** Temperament.

224 **For happy though but ill, for ill not worst** Though bad in terms of happiness, nevertheless not the most miserable possible.

Lines 229–83 Mammon speaks

Mammon means 'wealth'. He takes Belial's argument further. He agrees that there is no future in fighting God; nor would it help matters if God should:

> relent
> And publish grace to all on promise made
> Of new subjection,

since subjection, to them, is intolerable. He mocks the life of Heaven – an easy thing to do since it is very difficult to imagine Heaven as anything other than extremely boring. So he envisages the 'warbled hymns' and 'Forced Hallelujahs'. He identifies 'service' with 'servility'.

His solution is to 'seek our own good from our selves'; he thinks it possible to make Hell a passable imitation of Heaven. They have the 'gems and gold'; they have the 'skill or art'; they can 'raise/Magnificence; and what can Heaven show more?' While Mammon was in Heaven, it will be remembered, he never raised his eyes from the golden pavements, and he thinks that Heaven consists entirely in expensive eternals. He thinks that misery can be removed by spending money. He urges 'peaceful counsels and the settled state of order', again imitating the Heaven he so much despises. Belial at least admitted that in reconciling himself to Hell he was accepting something greatly inferior to Heaven; Mammon thinks that they can imitate Heaven so successfully that they won't be able to tell the difference.

231 **we then/May hope** i.e. never.
234 **The former** i.e. to unthrone the King of Heaven.
235 **The latter** To regain our lost rights.
242 **warbled** Sarcastic, like what follows.
250 **by leave obtained/Unacceptable** Even if God allowed us to become his servants again, we don't want to.
264 **Thick clouds and dark** See Psalm 18 – 'Clouds and darkness are round about him'.
271 **Want not** Does not lack.
278 **sensible** Sense.
281 **Compose** Arrange.

Lines 284–416 Beëlzebub proposes the master plan

The assembled devils, fear overcoming pugnacity, are persuaded to vote for peace. But Satan has a plan which will get the best of all worlds – 'revenge' of a kind, 'ignoble ease' for the rank and file devils, and glory for himself. He uses Beëlzebub as his mouthpiece. With all the bearing of an elder statesman at a solemn moment in history, Beëlzebub rises to his feet and propounds the solution to all their problems.

First, Beëlzebub sarcastically demolishes the idea that they can have peace. The only peace available to them is

> custody severe,
> And stripes, and arbitrary punishment,

so he proposes an 'easier enterprise' than a direct assault on God, the attack on newly-created Man. If they can't attack God Himself, at least they can vandalize His garden. Beëlzebub can be seen rubbing his hands with relish at the prospect:

> This would surpass
> Common revenge ...
> ... when his darling sons
> Hurled headlong to partake with us, shall curse
> Their frail original, and faded bliss,
> Faded so soon.

There is no more vivid expression of the devils' motto, 'Evil, be thou my good'. 'Faded bliss/Faded so soon' echoes with pathos, though for Beëlzebub it is triumph, the triumph of petty spite. The devils hate to see other people happy.

Satan and Beëlzebub both know that they can't, in fact, hurt God, that 'their spite still serves/His glory to augment', but choose to forget the fact. They spend their time cutting off their noses to spite their faces.

The great question still remains – to which Beëlzebub, of course, knows the answer:

> whom shall we send
> In search of this new world?

and, lest there should be too many volunteers, he emphasizes the danger and the difficulty, the near-impossibility of the enterprise:

> who shall tempt with wandering feet
> The dark, unbottomed, infinite abyss ...
> ... on whom we send
> The weight of all and our last hope relies.

288 **o'erwatched** Tired with lack of sleep.
292 **field** Of battle.
294 **the sword of Michaël** The two-handed sword with which Michael defeated the rebellious angels. 'Michaël' has three syllables.
296 **nether** Lower.
297 **policy** Clever, subtle statesmanship.
302 **front** Brow.
306 **Atlantean** Like Atlas, who held up the sky.
312 **style** Title.
313 **for so** i.e. judging by the applause which Mammon's speech had received.
315 **doubtless** Heavily sarcastic. Very likely!
329 **What sit we then** Why do we sit, then? 'Project' had a pejorative sense in Milton's day, implying something dishonest or absurd.
330 **determined** Put an end to, crushed.

332 **Vouchsafed or sought** Offered or asked for.

336 **to our power** To the limit of our power.

337 **reluctance** Resistance.

341 **Nor will occasion want** Nor will the opportunity be lacking.

346 **fame** Rumour, report.

361 **left/To their defence who hold it** i.e. left to men alone to defend.

367 **puny** Meant 'weak' or 'little', as now; but its primary and appropriate meaning was 'born since'.

375 **Their frail originals** Adam; or possibly 'their original happiness'.

376 **Advise** Consider.

382 **confound** Utterly ruin.

383 **one root** Adam.

391 **Synod** Meeting – usually in an ecclesiastical sense.

395 **those bright confines** The frontiers of Heaven.

404 **tempt** Try.

406 **the palpable obscure** Darkness which may be *felt*.

407 **uncouth** Strange, unknown.

409 **the vast abrupt** Chaos, the gulf between Hell and the world.
    arrive Reach.

412 **stations** Guards.

415 **Choice in our suffrage** Care in choosing by vote whom to send.

Lines 417–505 Satan volunteers

Not surprisingly, all the devils:

> sat mute,
> Pondering the danger with deep thoughts.

Satan, master of theatrical effect, leaves precisely the right length of pause before rising to his feet:

> with monarchal pride,
> Conscious of highest worth.

He secures maximum credit to himself by describing in vivid terms the perils that lie in his way before coming to his offer, with chest-swelling emphasis on the first person pronouns:

> But I should ill become this throne, O peers,
>   ... if aught proposed
> And judged of public moment, in the shape
> Of difficulty or danger could deter
> Me from attempting.

The emphasis on 'Me' is superb, the climax of the whole contrived dramatic scene. Satan begins and ends with 'Me'.

After a little flattery Satan urges the devils to entertain themselves as best they can while he is away and escapes before anybody can have the opportunity to offer to share the glory with him: they would have to be refused, but they would acquire some cheap glory.

Satan shows courage here, but the courage is motivated by malice and spite and the desire for power and glory. Milton points out that:

> for neither do the spirits damned
> Lose all their virtue; lest bad men should boast
> Their specious deeds on earth, which glory excites,
> Or close ambition varnished o'er with zeal.

There is a clear reminiscence here of St Paul's saying in Ephesians 2, 8 and 9: 'For by grace are ye saved through faith, and not of yourselves: it is the gift of God; not of works, lest any man should boast'.

The united devils rejoice in their 'matchless chief' and Milton ends the section with some rather ponderous moralizing on the disunity of man.

417 **expectation held/His look suspense** He stayed looking at them in expectation of a reply.
423 **Astonished** Struck with dismay.
425 **proffer** Offer himself, volunteer.
434 **convex** Vault.
439 **unessential** Having no existence.
441 **that abortive gulf** Reducing to non-existence.
448 **moment** Importance.
450 **Wherefore** Why?
452 **Refusing to accept** If I refuse to accept. He must accept as much danger as honour. Responsibility goes with power.
457 **intend** Consider.
461 **deceive** Beguile.
464 **coasts** Regions.
467 **prevented** Forestalled.
468 **lest, from his resolution raised** Lest others, encouraged by his resolution, should offer themselves, knowing that they would be refused but thereby getting a cheap reputation for valour.
478 **awful** Full of awe, respect.
485 **close** Secret.
490 **element** Sky.
492 **If chance** If it happens that.

Revision questions on lines 1–505

1 How does Beëlzebub's speech (310–78) prepare the audience for Satan's words (beginning line 390)?

2 Lines 488–95 are an example of an extended simile or comparison (likening the clearing of a storm to the renewed hope the devils obtain from their leader). Find examples of other extended images (for instance, in Book I, lines 200–8 in which Satan is compared to a whale, or lines 768–75 where the fallen devils are likened to a hive of bees). Show how Milton develops points of contact between the image and the situation which gave rise to it (e.g., the size of the whale, its capacity to deceive sailors, are obvious links to the figure of Satan). Try to assess the value of these similes, the extent to which they contribute to the tone or mood of the places where they appear in the poem.

Lines 506–628 The devils disperse

Satan enjoys his moment of glory surrounded by admiring supporters, until the devils disperse to beguile the time as best they can until Satan's return. Life in Hell is a meaningless succession of hours. Each devil – for despite their recent show of unity there is no real community in Hell – is searching for 'Truce to his restless thoughts'. Key words are 'Wandering', 'perplexed', 'restless'. Some hold their own Olympic games; others, with vast, frustrated energy to burn off, 'Rend up both rocks and hills'; others sing, but find nothing better to sing about than 'Their own heroic deeds and hapless fall', though their harmony, at least temporarily, 'suspended Hell'; others hold discussion groups, reasoning:

> Of providence, foreknowledge, will and fate,
> Fixed fate, free will, foreknowledge absolute

(note how the circular nature of their discussions is mimed), and like many of their earthly successors who engage in this pastime:

> found no end, in wandering mazes lost;

others go exploring the geography of Hell, which gives Milton the opportunity to describe more fully the desolation of the place where they find no rest, merely emptiness, nothingness:

> Rocks, caves, lakes, fens, bogs, dens, and shades of death,
> A universe of death, which God by curse
> Created evil, for evil only good,
> Where all life dies, death lives, and nature breeds,
> Perverse, all monstrous, all prodigious things,

Milton intended the whole passage, no doubt, as a parody of the way human beings in a fallen world pass their time and try to make their lives tolerable. He believed that nothing was satisfying or enduring – not even his beloved music – which wasn't in the service of God. Hell is full of 'Chimeras dire'; all is fantasy, illusion, nightmarish paradox.

506 **Stygian** Hellish.
508 **Paramount** Lord.
512 **globe** A compact band.
513 **emblazonry** i.e. their shields were covered with heraldic designs.
     horrent Bristling.
517 **alchemy** The trumpets were made of a brass alloy which looked like gold but was – like much else in Hell – imitation.
522 **ranged** Assembled in ranks. Ranged has two syllables.
523 **several** Separate.
526 **entertain** While away.
528 **sublime** Aloft, uplifted.
530 **the Olympian games or Pythian fields** The Greek games were held at Olympia and at Delphi, in honour of Apollo, the Pythian god.
531 **shun the goal** Steer as closely as possible round posts in chariot races.
532 **fronted Brigads** Opposing teams.
535 **van** Vanguard.
536 **Prick** Ride.
538 **welkin** Sky, upper air.
539 **Typhoean** 'Typhon' means whirlwind.
542 **Alcides** Hercules. The story alluded to was briefly this: Hercules, returning home to Trachis from Oechalia, where he had been victorious, sent Lichas to fetch a white robe in which he could sacrifice to Zeus. His wife sent a robe dipped in what she thought was a love-potion which would ensure that Hercules was faithful to her; but the potion was poisonous and when he put it on it stuck to his skin and he couldn't remove it. In agony he threw Lichas into the sea, climbed Mount Oeta in Thessaly, made a pile of wood and was burnt on it.

551 **Virtue** Strength.
552 **partial** Prejudiced in favour of themselves.
554 **Suspended** Held rapt.
   took Enchanted.
564 **Passion and apathy** Feeling and non-feeling. The Stoics
   believed in being insensible to feeling and suffering.
570 **gross** Tightknit, compact.
576 **baleful** Sorrowful.
577 **Styx** The word is derived from a Greek word meaning 'to
   hate'.
578 **Acheron** The stream of misery.
579 **Cocytus** The stream of wailing.
580 **Phlegeton** Means 'wailing'.
583 **Lethe** Lethe is set apart from the other four rivers. The
   word means 'forgetting'. When the dead drank from it they
   forgot their earthly lives, but the river rolls 'far off' and the
   devils can't obtain 'oblivion' from it.
591 **pile** Building.
592 **that Serbonian bog** Lake Serbonis is a dried-up lake in
   Lower Egypt between Damietta and Mount Casius. At times
   it filled up with sand. A Persian army once marched into it
   and sank.
594 **parching** Drying and withering with cold.
595 **frore** Frosty.
596 **harpy-footed Furies** Furies were avenging goddesses.
   Harpies were female monsters with wings, and they had
   hooked talons on their feet.
597 **revolutions** Seasons.
600 **starve** Perish with cold.
604 **sound** An estuary or strait.
610 **Fate withstands** Fate will not allow it to happen.
611 **Medusa** One of the three Gorgons. She was so ugly that
   anyone who looked at her was turned to stone.
614 **Tantalus** Tantalus was punished in Hades with a raging
   thirst. He was bound in a lake whose waters receded
   whenever he tried to drink from them. Hence 'tantalize'.
615 **forlorn** Lost.
625 **prodigious** Unnatural, monstrous.
628 **Hydras** The hydra was a huge snake with nine heads.
   Chimeras The chimera was a fire-breathing monster with
   three heads, part lion, part dragon, part goat.

Lines 629–870 Satan's journey. He meets Sin and Death

Satan reaches the nine-fold gates of Hell. There he encounters
Sin and Death. The following passage is a study in monstrous

grotesqueness and unnaturalness, reflecting the belief that evil, however speciously attractive it may make itself appear, is essentially ugly. Sin:

> seemed woman to the waist, and fair,
> But ended foul in many a scaly fold
> Voluminous and vast, a serpent armed
> With mortal sting:

see 1 Corinthians, 15, 56: 'the sting of death is sin'. At her waist she has a 'cry of hell hounds' which at times crept into her womb where they 'barked and howled/Within unseen'. She appears beautiful and alluring, but is also revolting and contains her own punishments within herself. Death is a mere threatening shadow until after the Fall, wearing 'the likeness of a kingly crown' against the day when he will be – or seem to be – lord of all things.

Satan, Sin and Death are the infernal Trinity which match the divine Trinity. The relation between the three of them is Milton's invention, though it is a development of the myth of Athena's birth from Zeus's head and an elaboration of the Epistle of James, 1, 15: 'When lust hath conceived it bringeth forth sin: and sin, when it is finished, bringeth forth death'. At the moment of Satan's 'bold conspiracy against heaven's King', Sin, a 'goddess armed', sprang forth from his head in a kind of nasty Virgin Birth. Sin was 'shining heavenly fair' and Satan seduced her incestuously. While Sin was pregnant, Satan was expelled from Heaven. Sin bore Death in a monstrously painful birth which distorted her 'nether shape'. She ran away, but Death pursued her and 'in embraces forcible and foul' raped her, producing the dogs which, in their turn, hourly rape her and gnaw her bowels. The passage is a horrible allegory of the incestuous relationship of Satan, Sin and Death, a grim *La Ronde* of lust and pain. Pleasure turns instantly to agony and creativity creates only destruction.

When Satan learns the identity of Sin and Death he becomes the smooth courtier again, speaking, with ghastly inappropriateness, of

> my fair son ... the dear pledge
> Of dalliance had with thee in Heaven.

He explains how his mission is to liberate them

> From out this dark and dismal house of pain,

presenting himself as a conquering hero. Sin envisages herself as sitting

> At thy right hand voluptuous

in hideous parody of the Son sitting at God's right hand.

629 **Adversary** Satan's name means 'adversary'.
632 **Explores** Tries out.
635 **concave** Roof.
637 **Hangs in the clouds** i.e. seems from a distance to be in the clouds.
     equinoctial winds The trade winds. Milton was thinking of a fleet of East Indiamen.
638 **Bengala** Bengal.
639 **Ternate and Tidore** Two of the spice islands of the Malay Archipelago.
640 **flood** Sea.
641 **Ethiopian** The Indian Ocean.
     Cape Of Good Hope.
642 **stemming** Pressing forward, breasting the waves.
647 **impaled** Fenced in.
652 **Voluminous** Literally, 'in rolls or folds'.
653 **mortal** Bringing death.
654 **cry** Pack.
655 **Cerberean** Cerberus was the dog with three heads who guarded Hades.
659 **abhorred** To be abhorred.
660 **Scylla** The legend is that Circe threw magic herbs into the water where Scylla bathed, with the result that dogs grew out of her womb.
661 **Calabria ... Trinacrian** Calabria is in Southern Italy; Trinacria is in Sicily.
662 **the night-hag** Hecate, the goddess of sorcery.
     called Invoked to take part in rites.
664 **the smell of infant blood** Witches were thought to be responsible for the death of infants.
665 **Lapland witches** Lapland was traditionally a centre of witchcraft.
     labouring Disturbed.
666 **Eclipses at their charms** The moon was thought to be affected by witchcraft.
671 **Furies** Avenging goddesses.
672 **dart** Javelin.
677 **admired** Wondered.

686 **taste** i.e. taste the results of.

688 **Goblin** Evil spirit.

693 **Conjured** Sworn together.

696 **reck'n'st thou** Do you count yourself among the spirits of Heaven?

706 **deform** Hideous.

709 **Ophiuchus** A northern constellation – 'the serpent-bearer'. Milton may be thinking of a comet which appeared in 1618. It was supposed to have caused the Thirty Years' War.

710 **horrid hair** Bristling tail.

716 **the Caspian** A notoriously stormy sea.

721 **like** Likely. The greater foe, of course, was Christ, who harrowed hell.

729 **bend** Aim.

730 **and know'st for whom** Do you know who will be pleased if you kill your father?

735 **Pest** Plague. The word 'pest' is weak, even comic, today, but in the seventeenth century was associated with the dreaded pestilence.

742 **first met thou call'st/Me father** The first time we have met you call me father.

755 **on the left side** As Athene sprang from the head of Zeus. There is a parody of Eve's creation from Adam's rib.

772 **pitch** Height.

784 **my nether shape** Sin was snakes from the waist down.

813 **mortal dint** Deadly blow.

815 **lore** Lesson.

818 **the dear pledge/Of dalliance** The sign of our love-making.

825 **pretences** Claims, designs.

829 **unfounded** Having no base, bottomless.

833 **purlieus** Outskirts.

834 **to supply/Perhaps our vacant room** To fill up the space we have left.

836 **surcharged** Overfull.

837 **broils** Wars.

842 **buxom** Yielding, pliant. The transition from its past to its present meaning makes an interesting study!
embalmed Made fragrant.

847 **famine** Hunger.

848 **Destined** Devoted.

849 **bespake** Spoke to.

859 **office** Duty.

Lines 871–1055 Satan journeys through Chaos and Night until he is in sight of earth

Sin opens the gates of Hell, using the key which is the 'sad instrument of all our woe' (and cf. Book I, line 3). The gates can now never be closed: they allow free passage out and in. In line 1025 Sin and Death build a bridge between Hell and earth:

> by which the spirits perverse
> With easy intercourse pass to and fro.

When Satan had made the original journey the rest was easy. Looking out from Hell, Sin and Satan see the boundless space of 'eldest Night/And Chaos'. This is an 'Illimitable ocean without bound' where:

> length, bredth and highth
> And time and place are lost.

Chaos and Night are the 'ancestors of Nature', the stuff from which God, by His word, created the ordered world of Nature. They have to be conveyed largely in negatives: they are shapeless, timeless, spaceless, lightless. Chaos is a place of endless war and meaningless noise: the four elements and the atoms gyrate, war, bounce off one another as Chance dictates. It is anarchy, as opposed to the ordered monarchy of God's creation. Not surprisingly

> Into this wild abyss the wary fiend
> Stood on the brink of Hell and looked awhile
> Pondering his voyage

before he takes the plunge.

There follows a superb description of Satan's space-travel flight: the first impetus; the sudden descent as through an air-pocket; the rising again; the struggle through quicksand; the desperate but undaunted effort as he

> With head, hands, wings or feet pursues his way,
> And swims or sinks, or wades, or creeps, or flies.

The passage is clogged and dense with the effort of his journey.

In 'a universal hubbub wild' Satan meets the personification of all that is anarchic – Chaos, Night, Rumour, Chance, Tumult, Confusion, Discord – and, appropriately since it is these things that he hopes to spread by reducing earth to 'universal darkness and your sway', he asks for guidance from them. Chaos's face is 'incomposed' – a non-face, like something from a horror film. He speaks feebly and inconsequently, but directs Satan, with good wishes, to

> another world
> Hung o'er my realm, linked in a golden chain
> To that side Heaven from whence your legions fell.

After more travail – harder, we are told, than the great journeys of myth – Satan comes near his journey's end. 'The sacred influence of light appears'; 'nature first begins/Her farthest verge'. The journey becomes easier and Satan can rest a moment 'at leisure to behold/Far off the empyreal heaven' and 'fast by hanging in a golden chain/This pendant world'. The earth is a jewel which he goes to steal. His pause is only momentary. Then

> Thither full fraught with mischievous revenge,
> Accursed, and in a cursed hour he hies.

889 **redounding** Surging in clouds.
891 **hoary** Grey with age.
895 **ancestors of Nature** The world was created out of Chaos. Nature is the created universe.
898 **Hot, Cold, Moist and Dry** The four elements from which all things were supposed to be made.
900 **embryon** Embryo.
904 **Barca ... Cyrene** Towns in Libya.
906 **To whom these most adhere,/He rules a moment** i.e. the element to which most atoms adhere is momentarily the winner.
911 **The womb of Nature and perhaps her grave** The world was created out of Chaos and may perhaps relapse into Chaos again.
913 **pregnant causes** Embryonic matter.
915 **them ordain** Puts them in order.
919 **frith** Channel, estuary, firth.
920 **pealed** Made to ring.
922 **Bellona** The goddess of war.
924 **this frame/Of Heaven** The structure of our sky.
926 **her axle** The earth's poles.
927 **vans** Wings.
937 **Instinct** Charged with.
     nitre Saltpetre. The thundercloud blows him upwards again.
939 **Syrtis** A quicksand near Tripoli.
941 **the crude consistence** The mixture of sea and land.
943 **gryphon** A hybrid of eagle and lion.
944 **moory** Marshy.

945 **the Arimaspian** The griffon was supposed to guard the goldmines of Siberia against the neighbouring Arimaspi.

948 **dense or rare** Matter which is dense at one moment, thin at another.

960 **pavilion** Large tent or encampment, or palace.

961 **wasteful** Desolate.

962 **sable-vested** Clothed in black.

964 **Orcus** Pluto, god of Hades.

965 **Demogorgon** An underworld god.

977 **Confine with** Border on.

988 **the Anarch** Chaos.

999 **if all I can will serve** If all I can do will help, staying here to defend what little is left to defend. Chaos is a confused speaker!

1001 **intestine broils** Civil wars.

1017 **Argo** The vessel in which Jason and the Argonauts sailed to capture the golden fleece. They sailed through the Bosphorous with its dangerous rocks.

1019 **Ulysses** Ulysses had to steer between Scylla and Charybdis, two monsters who guarded the Straits of Messina.
larboard The left side of a ship.

1029 **utmost orb** Outermost sphere.

1037 **Nature** The created universe as opposed to Chaos.

1043 **holds** Makes for.

1046 **Weighs** Rests on.

1050 **living** Vivid.

Revision questions on lines 506–1055

1 Discuss the dramatic qualities of Satan's encounter with Sin and Death at the gates of Hell.

2 Satan is, arguably, at his most heroic in the closing stages of Book II. Show how Milton, while acknowledging Satan's courage, guides and qualifies the reader's response so as to rule out a simple (and naive) approval of this character.

General questions and sample answers in note form

1 What does Satan's first speech (lines 84–124) reveal about his character and predicament?

2 What is the function of the parade of devils and pagan deities presented in the second half of Book I?

3 Describe the main stages in the debate before the intervention of Beëlzebub, and show how Milton exposes the flaws in the devils' arguments.

4 What is the function of the lines (506–628) describing the devils' activities as Satan sets out on his voyage to earth?

5 Comment on the dramatic qualities of the following speech from Book I:

>   Is this the region, this the soil, the clime,
> Said then the lost archangel, this the seat
> That we must change for heaven, this mournful gloom
> For that celestial light? Be it so, since he
> Who now is sovereign can dispose and bid
> What shall be right: farthest from him is best
> Whom reason hath equalled, force hath made supreme
> Above his equals. Farewell happy fields
> Where joy for ever dwells: hail horrors, hail
> Infernal world, and thou profoundest hell
> Receive thy new possessor one who brings
> A mind not to be changed by place or time.
> The mind is it own place, and in itself
> Can make a heaven of hell, a hell of heaven.
> What matter where, if I be still the same,
> And what I should be, all but less than he
> Whom thunder hath made greater? Here at least
> We shall be free; the Almighty hath not built
> Here for his envy, will not drive us hence:
> Here we may reign secure, and in my choice
> To reign is worth ambition though in hell:
> Better to reign in hell, than serve in heaven.
> But wherefore let we then our faithful friends,
> The associates and co-partners of our loss

> Lie thus astonished on the oblivious pool,
> And call them not to share with us their part
> In this unhappy mansion, or once more
> With rallied arms to try what may be yet
> Regained in heaven, or what more lost in hell?

6 Discuss Milton's poetic technique in the following excerpt from Book II.

>   At last his sail-broad vans
> He spreads for flight, and in the surging smoke
> Uplifted spurns the ground, thence many a league
> As in a cloudy chair ascending rides
> Audacious, but that seat soon failing, meets
> A vast vacuity: all unawares
> Fluttering his pennons vain plumb down he drops
> Ten thousand fathom deep, and to this hour
> Down had been falling, had not by ill chance
> The strong rebuff of some tumultuous cloud
> Instinct with fire and nitre hurried him
> As many miles aloft: that fury stayed,
> Quenched in a boggy Syrtis, neither sea,
> Nor good dry land: nigh foundered on he fares,
> Treading the crude consistence, half on foot,
> Half flying; behoves him now both oar and sail.
> As when a gryphon through the wilderness
> With wingèd course o'er hill or moory dale,
> Pursues the Arimaspian, who by stealth
> Had from his wakeful custody purloined
> The guarded gold: so eagerly the fiend
> O'er bog or steep, through straight, rough, dense, or rare,
> With head, hands, wings, or feet pursues his way,
> And swims or sinks, or wades, or creeps, or flies.

7 Why did Milton choose to begin *Paradise Lost* with Satan and the other devils in Hell? What does he gain by this opening?

8 What qualities do Satan and the other devils possess which might be called heroic? What comment does Milton make on these qualities?

9 Discuss those places in Books I and II where Milton reminds his readers that, although Satan 'reigns' in Hell, all his and the other devils' actions are performed with the 'high permission of all-ruling Heaven'. How effective are the author's interventions here?

10 'Reality was a scene too narrow for his mind' was the view of one of Milton's early critics and commentators. How far does Milton succeed in describing the indescribable – Hell, Sin, Death, Chaos?

11 How far can Satan be regarded as an accomplished actor?

12 Show how Milton uses Biblical, classical and mythological references in Books I and II. Decide whether a reference is there principally for its moral value or its appeal to our imagination.

13 'Milton's style in *Paradise Lost* is not natural; it is an exotic style. As his subject lies a good deal out of our world, it has a particular propriety in those parts of the poem.' Discuss.

14 'The reader finds no transaction in *Paradise Lost* in which he can be engaged; beholds no condition in which he can by any effort of imagination place himself; he has, therefore, little natural curiosity or sympathy.' Discuss.

15 Show how Milton distinguishes between the principal characters among the fallen angels both by what they say and how they say it.

16 To what extent does an appreciative reading of Books I and II depend upon the acceptance of the theology?

17 What aspects of Books I and II would make them suitable for dramatization (on film, or on stage)?

18 Comment on Milton's ability as a story-teller.

19 How would you persuade someone that it was worthwhile (even necessary!) to read *Paradise Lost* Books I and II?

Suggested notes for essay answers to questions 1–6

1 Satan must make an impact with his first spoken words in the poem. He has to show off his heroic qualities, but Milton requires the reader to see that Satan is also a figure flawed (on a grand scale) by pride and self-deception. His first words register the change in himself, indirectly, when he is scarcely able to recognize Beëlzebub, his principal accomplice in the revolt against Heaven. Satan doesn't dwell on change too long – to do so would not only be painful in itself but would also draw attention to the fact that what's occurred is primarily the speaker's fault. Instead, Satan looks to spread the blame: he emphasizes that they undertook together the task of over-throwing God (he and Beëlzebub were in '*mutual* league,/ *United* thoughts and counsels'). He falls back on the rather feeble excuse that his opponent was stronger than anticipated ('till then who knew/The force of those dire arms?'). Further self-justification follows – he acted out of 'high disdain', but the potential nobility of the motive is undermined by the fact that his scorn sprang from a 'sense of injured merit' (i.e., he felt hard done by). Having dealt with the uncomfortable matter of defeat Satan turns to the future, a prospect of glorious defiance and resistance to God – or, looked at another way, of futile posturing and refusal to face facts. Out of context Satan's determination to endure and defy sounds good – and it is difficult to withhold some admiration or sympathy from him, on occasions – but the negative foundations of his resistance ('revenge, immortal hate') should be noted. Above all, Satan isn't fighting for any cause which would dignify his stance – his cause is only, and entirely, himself. See also how he, absurdly, claims that they are somehow better off *because* of their defeat: 'In arms not worse, in foresight much advanced'. Now they know what they're up against. Yet Satan's first speech provides examples of selective blindness. 'Foresight' is precisely the quality he cannot afford if he is to continue to function as his absolute and egotistical self.

2 Such 'lists' are a familiar feature of epic poetry, and in *Paradise Lost* Milton was very deliberately producing a poem in the tradition of Greek and Roman epic works such as the *Iliad* or the *Aeneid*. Milton's aim was wider than that of his Greek or Latin predecessors; he wasn't telling the story of a siege or the founding of a nation, he was dramatizing the ultimate war (between God and Satan) and the creation of humankind. *Paradise Lost* therefore has a comprehensive, or encyclopedic, quality. It is the story of everything – or, in Milton's terms, everything that matters. The author must find a place in his narrative for the pagan gods which are scattered through the Old Testament, gods worshipped by the tribes around the Israelites and sometimes by the Israelites them-selves when they turned away from the true God. In the theology of Milton's time these pagan deities were the devils

cast out of Heaven after their revolt against God. They operated by fraud and cunning, and their corruption of the Israelites, God's chosen people, is an echo of the corruption of Adam and Eve, 'Man's first disobedience', the very heart of Milton's poem. In addition, Milton introduces the classical deities (Saturn, Jove), although the tone of these references is less severe than that applied to the Old Testament figures. In particular the description of the fall of Mulciber (Book I = lines 738–46) is given with a conscious grace, which Milton promptly crushes by pointing out (lines 748/9) that classical myth is actively wrong, misleading.

3 The first three speakers take up neatly differentiated positions, from Moloch's desperate do-or-die remedy to Belial's do-nothing solution, with Mammon's proposal that they should build a kind of substitute Heaven falling somewhere in between. Moloch's idea that they make an open attack on Heaven is literally suicidal, as he half acknowledges when he claims that if God is sufficiently incensed He will put the devils out of their misery. Belial says, in essence, that God might forget about them if they cause no trouble, do nothing – the very opposite of Moloch's maddened heroism. Ironically, Belial mocks those of his fellow devils who haven't the toughness to face the consequences of their actions (i.e., their perpetual confinement in Hell). But it is plain that Belial is terrified of provoking God into further punitive action. Mammon's argument that they should dress up disaster by erecting an alternative empire in Hell is the one that wins the approval of the audience, because it is neither as reckless as Moloch's plan nor as shamefully passive as Belial's suggestion. Mammon's words sound positive (making 'prosperous of adverse', etc.) but his vision is sadly limited: for him paradise is only a matter of gold-plated buildings.

4 The lines act as a bridge between Satan's acceptance of the mission and his beginning it. They allow Milton a pause in the narrative before the author embarks on the intrinsically more dramatic material of the climax of Book II. We have heard little of the mass of 'ordinary' devils; the focus has been on the leaders. Now Milton shows how the 'children' busy themselves when the father-figure of Satan is away on business. There is a poignant futility to their activities. They split into groups to play games or go off singly to vent their rage and frustration by tearing up 'both rocks and hills'. Some sing. Others debate (on an abstract level as opposed to the more practical nature of the debate at the beginning of Book II). Another group explores the dismal limits of Hell (Milton dwells on the dreariness and the torments of the place). These activities are futile because, like most pastimes, they don't get anywhere. The debaters, for instance, only get tangled up in their own words. At best the devils can hope to forget for a few moments that they live in Hell. But what the devils do has also a kind of poignancy or pathos to it – because their activities are so reminiscent of what we all do for greater or lesser stretches of our lives: play to distract ourselves, while away the time, avoid facing reality. This is perhaps the passage in Books I and II in which the devils appear most sympathetic to the reader.

5 The essence of drama is conflict, and Satan makes plain at once that he remains implacably hostile to God. If we stop and analyse it we see holes in his argument (how can Satan 'reign' in Hell when he has already admitted at the beginning of the speech that God – whom he refuses to name directly – is 'sovereign' and can do as He pleases?). But if we judge the speech as a *performance*, intended to hearten both himself and Beëlzebub, it works splendidly. It is carefully phrased in memorable, succinct lines ('Better to reign in hell, than serve in heaven'). After an opening sentence in which the speaker comments sadly on the change from Heaven to Hell (note the comparatively gentle, reflective tone here), we are confronted by the three blunt monosyllables – 'Be it so' – as Satan faces the truth that the change is irreversible. With histrionic or stagy phrasing he even seems to welcome the prospect: 'Hail horrors, hail/Infernal world . . .'. He is constantly striking new poses: the proud possessor of a new kingdom; the individual unbowed by defeat; the considerate leader mindful of 'our faithful friends'.

6 Milton makes full use of the dramatic potential of Satan's voyage (or flight?) through Chaos. At the same time he must keep before us the fact that Satan is a *malign* spirit, and that ultimately we should wish him not to succeed. Milton diminishes Satan by putting him at the mercy of the elements he is crossing. The passage begins boldly as the devil climbs after take-off. Note the open 'a' sounds ('As in a cloudy chair ascending rides/Audacious') which suggest the expansive confident nature of the flight. However, like a cartoon character who realizes too late that he is walking on thin air, Satan suddenly plummets. His undignified fall (echoing, on a comic level, his earlier fall from Heaven) is enacted through Milton's choice of language and the (absence of) punctuation. The over-run lines and the alliteration of

> all unawares
> Fluttering his pennons vain plumb down he drops
> Ten thousand fathom deep

demand that the verse be read in a breathless gulp. (See, by contrast, the last three lines of this excerpt. It is impossible to read those quickly.) Satan's rescue from a perpetual fall was a matter of chance ('*ill* chance' as far as we are concerned) and the way in which Milton has him blown 'many miles aloft' by an explosive cloud emphasizes the point that Satan has no control over his destiny, or even his destination. As he becomes bogged down in his journey so too does the verse turn plodding ('nigh foundered on he fares'). And just as it is impossible to define the nature of the element(s) that Satan is forcing a way through, so does Milton find it impossible to give a single name to his movement (he 'swims or sinks, or wades, or creeps, or flies' – each verb is given an identical weight).

Further reading

C. S. Lewis, *A Preface to Paradise Lost* (Oxford University Press, 1960).

C. Ricks, *Milton's Grand Style* (Oxford University Press, 1978).

L. Potter, *Preface to Milton* (Longman, 1986).